Tatt
I love U
for all your
continued support.
— Jan

Tetiania,
Thank you!!!
Flowers are amazing!!
ABDUL

This page is intentionally left blank.

First Printing, 2015

Book designed and published by Accomplice, LLC

ISBN 978-0-692-51725-3

SINCERELY ME

sincerely me

Abdul Raoof I. Hamidullah

Lawrence E. B. Nicol

Accomplice, LLC

In loving memory of

George Samuel Remilekun Nicol

Table of Contents

The Challenge

How to Lose Your Mind

Love

Woman's Understanding

Manhood

Perfect Eyebrows

These Lonely Nights

Time

Vicissitudes

WIM

Pretty on the Inside

Worms and Dust

Faith

American Smile

The Curse

Walk

The Opaque

Ought to Quit

Does There Have to be a Reason?

Pulse

Breathtaking

The Devil Laughs

Don't Shoot

Brooklyn Snow White

It's Not Yours

3 Deep Breaths

Unsuccessful

Lo Siento

My Maybe Tree

More Time

The Word

Feeling Lifeless

Symmetry of Love

Childhood Memories

A Love Song

So You Understand

Lupita Elba

End of a Beautiful Era

Carved In Stone

Gentlenigga

Lover's Slavery

My Nina Mosely

Who Will Intervene?

Would You Believe?

Post 365

Love Bomaye

For me, this book started as a way to push a friend into sharing his talents with the world without fear. Little did I know that I would end up placing bits of my mind, heart, soul on display. I am grateful for this experience and friendship.

-Abdul Raoof I. Hamidullah

Challenge

Perhaps the mirror is not enough?

Maybe it takes someone else to see the best that

sits within me?

Seated behind insecurities.

Row behind row.

Tucked away from the aisles of life

Staring at an empty stage.

At this stage of life my fight is within,

But maybe that's not enough?

To face my face when I face my fears

To spar and joust when no one is near.

Sure of myself that I by myself

Can make a better me.

Maybe I can't see myself when I gaze into this

glass and ask...

Am I the best to be?

Perhaps I need someone else to see the best that

sits within,

Hiding behind rows and rows of insecurities.

Maybe I need a sparring partner?

Maybe I need...a challenge!

-Abdul Raoof I. Hamidullah

How to lose your mind

To lose one's home is bad enough.

...but it's never only that.

Along slides a voice,

Then everything overlooked:

Toilets, showers, tables, and shelter.

The ties of kith and kin wear thin,

And bend and break.

But the human voice is the hardest loss.

The words we say just to say.

To be polite, or true, or rude.

To disappear and melt into the air we breathe.

Unseen. Unspoken. Unheard

...but it's never only that.

The voice we speak within our souls

To get through every day.

Our plans, our thoughts, hopes and dreams

Kept close within our breast.

Not hearing the simple sound of another human

voice will drive you mad!

'till once your breast is cracked and crushed.

Then conversations rush

To your ears.

...but from your own tongue.

-Abdul Raoof I. Hamidullah

Love

A baby's frantic scream

When mother walks away.

The silent comfort upon her return.

A father's fearful cringe

At sound of such a scream.

The sigh of relief that all is well.

A thoughtful friend consistent to a fault.

The grateful kindness of friendship's bond.

A hopeful heart that blindly leads the mind.

The understanding of memories that linger.

A desperate prayer responded just in time.

The faith that grows and fills the heart with joy.

A fragile voice exposed in hushed anxiety.

The strength of forgiveness and fellow
vulnerability.

A gift from God to give and give again.

This is love.

-Abdul Raoof I. Hamidullah

A Woman's Understanding

The final thin wet bead traces her cheek.

Soft and cool.

No hurt nor laughter.

A simple sigh.

A lesser burden.

A heart relieved.

A woman's understanding.

-Abdul Raoof I. Hamidullah

Manhood

He is not his lustful heart.

Nor his confidence of mind.

But faith to grasp the reins of both

So closely intertwined.

So thoughtful he neglects himself.

Yet builds himself the same.

For sake of other than his own

Unmentioned only shown.

He utters words restrained.

No anger overcomes.

Nor pardon for his failures

Lest they remain undone.

He often bows his soul in truth

Not just in desperation.

He leans upon the throne eternal

Accepting many burdens.

He is gracious and unyieldingly inhales the stench

of fear.

Yet shrinks away from glory when it's handed out

by men.

For manhood is no easy task.

Not clear for all to see.

But since childhood it's been my path,

The only path for me.

-Abdul Raoof I. Hamidullah

Perfect Eyebrows

Short skirts and straight hair.

Low cut tops and legs comfortably crossed in a

crowded club.

Meticulously made up faces

Devoured by the prowling eyes of thirsty wolves.

Photocopied reality of celebrity selfies' filtered IG

posts,

#nofilter.

Imaginary conversations and short messages

rapidly thumbed into existence.

But beneath the foundation lies tension.

The elegant beauty of a blemish

Buried below perception.

The hope to bear her soul and life in a single

breath.

Mingling through a breadth of singles insecure in

their own souls.

And so it goes...

The hidden pain and trust betrayed.

Loyalty lost as time unfolds.

Attention to details.

Waxed, threaded, and plucked flawlessly, then... a

smile of self contentment

Perfect eyebrows!

All the while neglecting the subtle elegance of a

wild strand.

-Abdul Raoof I. Hamidullah

These Lonely Nights

When all are sleep and silence rolls

With a deafening roar.

Slumber creeps through a creaky door,

But slips away as eye lids raise.

Time is slow, fighting fierce and

Slumber stays away.

My mind is trained and flesh confused.

Foolish hope that I command

What time of day,

And place that I shall sleep.

-Abdul Raoof I. Hamidullah

Time

Time presses forward.

Memories float in its wake.

With questions from the past

Of directions it could take.

To reflect is just a waste.

And what's worse to waste than time?

Time presses forward,

But backwards in the mind.

-Abdul Raoof I. Hamidullah

Vicissitudes

Beyond control, the tides of time

Gather lives in the undertow.

Swept away then cast ashore

To unfamiliar sands.

Beyond the reach of charted paths

Do time and distance span.

Some souls are meant to intertwine,

And some stand side by side.

Others merely steal a glance,

And worse is some collide.

Where do we land when tides retreat,

And froth is washed away?

And maps have torn our hearts to scorn

The journeys we have set.

Some friends were never meant to be,

Some friends are not enough.

The pulse of life will overwhelm

Then dare you not to touch.

The bond of love too vigorous

But less the committed tongue.

Buried in the barren sand

Beneath the burning Sun.

Till next there comes a wave to crash and gather

what was lost.

Or simply toss across the sea again

Amongst the froth.

-Abdul Raoof I. Hamidullah

WIM

I look in the mirror and see myself in sharp

details.

I see my strengths and my faults.

My scars and my pain.

My smiles and my joy,

We're both the same.

Our movements match,

My heart is one.

I reach to touch and embrace but fail.

Then I realize...there is no glass before me.

But another soul.

That I cannot hold nonetheless.

-Abdul Raoof I. Hamidullah

Pretty on the Inside

She wears makeup sometimes,

But doesn't need to.

Fills the air with sweet aroma,

But just a touch.

Well dressed and groomed,

Impeccable to the eye.

But none of this stays in the mind.

Boys see her skin eager to touch.

Missing the essence,

Essentially missing much.

Within her smile is an unseen.

Conversations are effortless.

She even speaks in silence.

Only a man can appreciate,

Especially the blind.

Within her breast is a heart.

Behind her face, a mind.

Girls imitate the physical.

In adoration of her honor.

But worthless is her beauty,

If she's not pretty on the inside.

-Abdul Raoof I. Hamidullah

Worms and Dust

Worms and dust wait with souls from centuries
past

Solemn flowers

Fond memories and

Prayers on their behalf

No wealth nor flesh can follow

This path of deeds behind

To work in its stead

Clinging to life's bed as I climb

Time races ahead

Regretting the seconds that dash

Sprinting off my heels

As present drifts to past

The future is here

The end unknown

But I cannot ignore what mustn't last

For it takes a lifetime for this flash.

Worms and dust yearn to wait with me tomorrow.

At laughter's last alas my solemn sorrow.

What love did I leave?

What time did I spend?

What deeds do I have to redeem?

Not for my flesh

But my wait with worms and dust,

Memories, flowers, and prayers.

-Abdul Raoof I. Hamidullah

Faith

I've never seen the gates of hell nor smelled it's
wicked stench.

Nor have mine eyes felt the might of paradise.

How easy it is to stain my heart with sins life has
to offer

And tread the earth in misery hopelessly towards
my coffin.

But in this darkened place that feels God forsaken

Is every breath I breathe and all that I have taken.

My breath is not yet halted and heart still pounds
with strength.

No choice have I nor you left but to learn, fight,
and live.

Perhaps someday soon I'll smell that wicked
stench,

And wish for days again on lands in life so
treacherous.

But maybe if I fight enough and supplicate in tears,

Mine eyes will glance the mercy of my lord for whom I fear.

-Abdul Raoof I. Hamidullah

American Smile

Don't smile at me with perfect teeth

And cheeks raised well rehearsed.

Unhappy lying fearful grin whenever you're

unnerved.

Disguised hatred racist mask that looks nice and

sweet.

The caution sign of sinister motives of certainty.

Your anger shows the truth,

And grief can tell no lie.

Happiness brings laughter,

So what then is this smile?

Deceit to grasp my purse?

To cause me calm before my slaughter?

Your undisputed innocence?

Your confidence of power?

The pain you hide and lock away

Till tears infuse your cheeks.

With tightened lips

And bright white teeth

Aligned in symmetry.

Don't smile at me with perfect teeth.

I trust not such a thing.

You hungry wolves which know no bounds

Corrupted heart unseen.

Your stolen shores and mountain tops.

Your pure white robes of terror.

Your compromising heart.

Your "absolutely" meaning never.

Don't raise your cheeks so well rehearsed

Though now it comes with ease.

To be polite or hide the truth,

Our simply just to please.

-Abdul Raoof I. Hamidullah

The Curse

With the deepest sincerity a curse was uttered

Then a call upon our lord.

Then another curse,

Condemning the unborn.

Out of frustration and anger.

And so I struggle to stand and break free from my

inclinations.

The parts of me I seek to improve but somehow

never do.

The things I hate when my parents look in my

eyes and see themselves.

The parts they feared

And hoped would never come to be.

That I disdained to see them display.

So here I am.

Confined to a curse of two generations.

How heavy the burden of repeated faults weighs

on the growing child.

And I spend my life to overcome

Driven by a curse of my own.

To never be the same when I am grown.

If we only paused to consider those fateful words:

"I hope you have children that are just like you".

-Abdul Raoof I. Hamidullah

Walk

Don't run into my arms.

Don't run away in haste.

Let not this moment fade

Faster than remaining days.

Take slowly measured steps.

At an everlasting pace.

If fate should be so cruel

Let it languish in its place.

May you have the best of life.

May your days be filled with joy.

May your patience and your faith remain and

never leave a void.

May your ending be as passionate

And hopeful as the start.

If we are to be forgotten,

May were echo in our hearts.

Should we hurry to begin?

Or rush to meet the end?

Or stand and feel the floral scents

Within the gentle wind?

So I'll walk and take all day.

Many others pass me by.

No desire for the chase

Nor wander of the eye.

The first blossom to burst brings the shortest

sharpest bloom.

The thorn removed with speed is forgotten far

too soon.

If joy should be the goal

Let me view it from afar.

If pain the fate then let me

Walk with feet secured in tar.

-Abdul Raoof I. Hamidullah

The Opaque

Destiny lurks behind walls of darkness.

Ready to pounce

And rip to shreds the well thought out

And nudge the course of life.

Fate lies hidden within the path

To twist and turn destined hearts

Massaging minds into accepting final

destinations.

Fortune comes and goes as planned.

For gains and loss unknown to man.

Despite best efforts and worst dealt hands.

Transforming lives throughout the lands.

Providence guides all things unseen.

With rules and laws meted out.

In perfect order misunderstood

Lest faith should leave the heart and die in minds

that overcome.

Until the end.

Succeed or fail.

Unmasking death's visage once veiled.

As proof he must prevail.

-Abdul Raoof I. Hamidullah

Ought to Quit

When we met you said all the right things

I was amazed at how quickly you understood me

There were times I didn't have to say a word

You would just finish my sentences

That's how you hooked me.

Now I can't think straight and struggle to express

what I really feel

Alive? In love?

Love became lust

And every conversation took a dirty turn

I thought you'd learn

But you gave me less of what I wanted

I've told you so many times but you just don't

listen

And I heat to repeat myself!

I said I hate to repeat myself!

But there is something about you that keeps me

coming back

That makes me stay

Maybe it's too hard to go out alone?

Maybe it's because you still make me laugh?

And I have faith that one day you'll get it right.

Or maybe I'm just a fool.

Addicted to your confident touch

So I overlook your flaws and what to expect

As I share my closest thoughts

With you...

Autocorrect

-Abdul Raoof I. Hamidullah

Does There Have to be a Reason?

Does there have to be a reason when I check on
you at night?

And add you to my prayers?

Or when I call to mind?

Your face when I awake?

Or just before I nod?

Does there have to be a reason?

Other than ... Just because?

When a toddler gives a hug and rushes to
welcome home.

And teaches man the purity and truth of love
unknown.

No explanation given.

None needed just the same.

Seems meaningless to many,

To slowly speak your name,

And emulate the child

Until we come alive again.

Must we always justify with why?

Or is it just within?

-Abdul Raoof I. Hamidullah

Pulse

Lowly breaths and heartbeats rise.

Then race unwarned and unexpected.

Then flow in rhythms uncontrolled

Obsessed and un-neglected.

To dance with other breaths and beats

Whenever they do meet.

With gentle graceful smiles and tones

That ebb and flow with time.

At once it's gone then back again

In never ending spirals.

A spinning head and racing breast

With lungs of life

...and lifelessness.

In deeper distant patterns.

So hearts can feel

And fill 'till full,

And breaths do quickly calm

Inviting comfort and peace of mind

When blood doth pump away.

-Abdul Raoof I. Hamidullah

Breathtaking

'twas not the beauty eyes beheld

That caused hearts to swell

And thoughts to drift away from grip

To fantasies withheld.

'twas not the smile that lit the flame

That brought hearts to change

And thoughts to wander endlessly

Burning deep within.

'twas not the kindness received

That filled hearts with ease

And thoughts of ways to do the same without
intent to gain.

But gratitude towards God I saw in every action
taken.

'twas life's burdens borne with grace

That brought about that smiling face, gentle hand
and beauty unmistaken.

-Abdul Raoof I. Hamidullah

The Devil Laughs

The devil grins and smirks

Then laughs

Overjoyed with his success.

The wedge he placed between

The pair that promised not to let.

But failed themselves just as

The first pair placed and given breath.

The smallest things became extreme

In minds he did affect.

Another promise within one's breast to grudge
quietly kept.

Soon the other followed.

The devil never rests.

He grins and smirks then laughs

Overjoyed with his success.

To split the bond between the pair

That promised not to let.

But failed themselves just as the

The first pair placed and given breath.

The wedge remained and so was pressed in minds
to gain more depth.

What was within now sits between

Unmoved because they slept.

The devil never rests.

He grins and smirks then laughs

Overjoyed with his success.

The laughs were heard as angry words and
grudges closely kept.

And screams and hurtful words

Intent to spread the pain they wept.

Tearful doves restrained their wings

'till peace was nowhere found.

The hateful hush of the overjoyed

Devil the only sound.

-Abdul Raoof I. Hamidullah

All these pieces came from my life experiences. Some good, some bad, some real bad. But through it all I was able to persevere and with that said I give you every bit of me in each piece. This journey was a long one with many ups and downs and moments where I doubted my ability to speak the truth through my words. Luckily I was able to find myself in poetry and I hope when you're done reading this you will be able to do the same.

-Lawrence E. B. Nicol

Don't Shoot (Stand for Something)

I see you're willing to stand for something.

But will you still raise your hands in protest?

When the news loses interest in the slaying of

young black boys?

Will you march in solidarity if there is no one to

document your movements?

See what are you really fighting for?

But the opportunity to say you were there?

When will enough be enough?

How much more blood will be shed in the name of

the law?

The very same law that swore to serve and

protect you.

What stories must you tell your child when you

send him off into this world?

A world that wants nothing more

Than to see him as a man who fits the description.

A description he often knows nothing about but

somehow was born with.

See this is my reality.

Somehow our melanin became a target

For those who harbor hatred for a race of men

who want nothing more than to be equals.

Equal enough to walk the streets and make it

home without

making a national headlines; black man slain

before his time.

See this is now becoming the norm

And we can no longer choose to ignore.

They are picking us off one by one,

Till we are no more.

I see you're willing to stand for something.

But please do more than raise your hands in
protest.

They say the revolution will not be televised.

Nor will it wait for those who stand on the
sidelines.

It is time to make a change.

Lift up your voices and be heard!

Let them know we are worth more than make

shift memorials and teddy bears on corners.

Liquor poured over concrete.

We have seen too many mothers mourning

And we are tired.

I am tired.

Tired that our lives mean little next to nothing

In a world where our legacies are forced to

scream martyrs for causes we choose not to die

for.

And to the next brother who won't make it home due to the unjust balance of power I pray to the almighty God your death will not be in vain.

And for those us who are left to remain to endure this pain I pray you do SOMETHING.

-Lawrence E. B. Nicol

Brooklyn Snow White

My health insurance doesn't cover heartbreaks.

Yet I'm still over here dying for you.

You buried my heart in your borough.

Never to return, a Queen of the city that

Never sleeps.

How ironic, I only catch you in my dreams.

When my slumber takes over me and its okay to

revisit the past.

Reliving the moments that once defined our

destiny.

Who would have known we'd part ways.

A love surreal and I'm not quite finished with

loving you yet.

Yet I know the space you've taken which severed

our love

Is what you needed to grow so who am I to hold

you back?

Knowing you'll never look back

And I'll never look forward.

Cause while you'll be wherever you are doing

whatever it is you'll be doing.

I'll be stuck here contemplating the "what ifs" and

"maybes".

Hoping it'll bring peace to my mind during these

trying times.

If I could only find the answer to your insecurities

If only I'd mirror my mistakes and correct them

beforehand

You'd be beside me more than through thick and

thin and my patience wouldn't feel

Like a death sentence instead a testimony to all

things written in stone,

My love for you is strong.

-Lawrence E. B. Nicol

It's Not Yours

I gave my heart to another.

Just to have her rest comfortably in the arms of

another man.

And that right there lets me know this world is full

of cruel jokes.

Every day I just wait for the punch line,

Or your call.

And I don't know what's worse that I'll never

Get it or I'll never get you again.

And they say you have to laugh to keep from

crying.

But I've never wept tears of sorrow.

How many men can say they loved a queen in

their lifetime?

So each tear will be a merry one.

Even though I did not marry you.

I was able to love a real woman, a real woman a real woman!

There must be comedic relief to this.

All this can't be life.

I even think about her before prayers and maybe that's my problem.

Maybe the prayers then she shall follow accordingly but the heart supersedes the brain, and...

And the heart wants what it wants.

-Lawrence E. B. Nicol

3 Deep Breaths

I took 3 deep breaths before I visited a memory In
which I loved you.

Things seem so simple when I inhale.
Past times flow through my body
Like I'd be living them right now if it wasn't for
you being miles away.
It's like Lauryn's looped in my head and the
Miseducation was a testament to the foundation
we built.
It could all be so simple, but we rather make it
hard.
So hard that I actually believed you.
That I actually believed I loved you myself
Thought trying times would add flavor to the
stories we'd tell our grandkids.

If only we had 3 more breathes together

Maybe we could reach for a fourth.

-Lawrence E. B. Nicol

Unsuccessful

I started to reconcile with the thought of

Losing you.

I remember a life where loving you consumed my

clock.

Tempted to revisit the past, I recite your words As

if kisses were forming an unspoken language.

Gently touching my lips are memories of a beauty

so phenomenal

That I'd be intoxicated with your presence.

I couldn't want to be anywhere but here in my

dreams.

Where you run freely through my mind

consuming all that is me.

I've battled with the decisions made

As I watched our hearts fade

And my nightmare came into existence.

There were few steps to take

But somehow we lost track of our footing.

And now you're there and I'm here.

Both wishing we were near.

But separated between pride and fear.

Never giving this a true chance at survival.

Only reminiscing on what a great love this could

have been.

Only if we would have spoken.

-Lawrence E. B. Nicol

Lo Siento

She said there were no more opportunities left To give.

I had robbed her of her innocence.

Spread her rose petals across the concrete in the name of lust.

How could she ever trust a man or take his Name when the time came.

See she was already a casualty to circumstance.

She said love never lived here,

Nor did it spend a night occasionally to let her know she was welcome.

All she could ever remember was the sound of the condom wrapper being torn.

The scent of sweat on my flesh.

And the fact I'd never say goodbye when I was done.

She became a martyr to a cause she wasn't Willing
to die for.

But somehow had given her life, in hopes that I'd
see that her testimony was one that would be
worthy to cry for.

I never knew a man's touch would mean so much
to a woman until I could never lay hands on her
again.

She fell victim to an unrequited love and
somehow I'm here playing the role of the
antagonist to a love story she could never tell.

-Lawrence E. B. Nicol

My Maybe Tree

Left hanging on this tree

Is all that's left of me?

I couldn't even feel this pain.

No choking.

No struggle.

Just a body lifelessly dwindling in the wind.

I came.

I saw.

I attempted to conquer.

But this world was too much for me.

These bullies they got the best of me

And I had nothing left to give.

So I grabbed this rope and called it quits.

Now that I'm gone maybe the world will miss my

poetry.

Maybe just one person will realize I'm gone.

Maybe, just maybe I wouldn't have to be hanging

from this tree...

If someone, if anyone would have loved ME.

-Lawrence E. B. Nicol

More Time

I wish we had more time...

Like clocks could stop.

We could stand in silence... And just be....

Embrace all that we, ever had to offer with just

the glance of our eyes....

They say that I should let you go.

That I should file these memories in places my

brain won't dare find courage to go.

They want me to forget you.

Act as if your existence was just something

fictional.

Like I dreamt you up one morning

After a bowl of cereal.

-Lawrence E. B. Nicol

The Word

My words made your heart sing like church choirs

on Easter Sunday.

How could something so miraculous not be

crafted by the hands of God?

I even thought I saw traces of his fingerprints on

the stitching of your frame.

His name taken in vain when we part ways.

God damn! Why would you tease me?

Forbidden fruit in the form of flesh.

This healthy obsession was so much more than

nourishment.

Yet still I'm dying for a taste of you

Like addicts after that first hit.

-Lawrence E. B. Nicol

Feeling Lifeless

Feeling lifeless, unable to breathe.

Knowing each breath could be your last.

Life's most humbling experience stuck.

Unwilling to compromise with mistakes you've

made.

Knowing they'd catch up with you somehow.

Dreading the realization that you aren't

Everything you've claimed to be.

No knight in shining armor.

Just tarnished dreams of making one's self Better.

See I could have loved you but I didn't learn to

Love myself so now we're stuck here figuring Out

how to salvage what's left of this Catastrophe.

And you just seem

Oh so mad at me that I'd gladly walk away to

Never witness you bare so much pain.

Cause my heart and mind can't take it.

I'm going insane and my sanity is all I have left.

Since what little love I had is buried in your

Pocket.

Sooooo far down that it seems to take months To

retrieve memories of you and I.

When things weren't perfect.

See they could never be perfect.

That's the reality of love.

But I've grown to know your worth.

-Lawrence E. B. Nicol

Symmetry of Love

We fell in line with the symmetry of love.

Backtracked our steps to where right met Wrong,

And still found time to dance the night away.

A collision with lust led you to believe such Things

should come to an end.

Couldn't help but fight the inevitable.

Society's perception of us made you think Twice.

But that third thought brought you closer to Me.

Like what would this world be if we never Existed

for one another?

You'd journal the plight of our downfall.

Hoping you could rewrite our history

While I'd just sit here in silence.

A perfect peace knowing I was blessed to have A

piece of you.

Even if it left me in pieces.

See I see you when I see myself.

So I know I'll never be alone.

And even when you're with him

For those few seconds I run across your mind.

Time stands still and we're together

Just how we're supposed to be.

So even with your imperfections they made You

Perfect.

I could recognize greatness in you. Wholeness.

You were complete before I met your

Acquaintance.

And maybe if I had positioned myself to do the

Same,

Things might be a little different.

Maybe this would last.

-Lawrence E. B. Nicol

Childhood Memories

Your love reminded me of my childhood

It's like the neighborhood lights came on

It's no longer time to play

Can I be serious with you...

I never thought I'd get here in a million years

See it's funny how time flies

Can I just glide with you

Soar into memories uncharted

Beyond boundaries of discomfort

I feel like I know you better than I know myself

Can I say prayer with you

Different religious backgrounds but we found love

in the name of God

Hallowed be thy name

Will you ever forgive me

I know practice makes perfect

How many tries will I get to get to you...

See there's no place I rather be than here

So stand close

And let no man come between what God destined

for us to be

Eternal lovers.

-Lawrence E. B. Nicol

A Love Song

I wanted to write you a love song

I remember Lauryn once told me the sweetest

thing ever known was like the kiss on the collar

bone

I wondered if she stared into your eyes while

watching the sun set

Now three years removed and I feel like you don't

know my name

I wish I could have practiced what I preached

Maybe then these Confessions wouldn't come

crashing in like wrecking balls

See I don't want to wait in vain for your love

But I know when a women's fed up

It ain't nothing you can do about it

And I'm so anxious to show you

These bad habits don't mean I can't understand a

woman's worth

So just let me love you for a couple of forevers

And even if that's not enough

And you find the sweetest taboo in him

I want you to remember we were friends turned

lovers

So you'll always be my latest and greatest

inspiration

And don't ever let it be a factor that I'm your ex

and have you thinking you don't ever have to call

Cause I don't want to tell Mr. Telephone man

there's something wrong with my line

So call me

Best friend of mine....

-Lawrence E. B. Nicol

So You Understand

They say absence makes the heart grow fonder

Or is it out of sight out of mind?

I just wanted to remind you that the man you

molded me to be would be considered a treasure.

Why let her steal your glory?

Your love was the next best thing to the second

coming of Jesus Christ.

And like his return I wait for you.

I'm sure before time it was written in

hieroglyphics.

That a woman as prolific as you would come to

change my life.

Forgive me for being dumb, deaf, and blind to

your vision.

And now that I'm calling, I'm hoping these rings

don't fall on deaf ears.

I rather place them on fingers to show the world

my commitment to you.

Let it be known. My body may have strayed but

my heart, which was yours from the start,

Has never wandered

They say what's understood between lovers need

not be explained and still I find myself telling you

things you Already knew I was yours before I

knew I was yours... And I forever will be.

So You Understand...

-Lawrence E. B. Nicol

Lupita Elba

I was taught my skin complexion was something I should be afraid of.

I was lead to believe beauty did not exist in my pigmentation.

The world would rid me of my innocence before I could even discover it.

So many shades to adore but somehow mine left to wither away as if black didn't matter.

As if I were a forgotten piece of the color spectrum, not even good enough for a rainbow.

Brainwashed to believe "if it ain't light it ain't right" so I held those who did not share my melanin in high regards. See they were royalty and I could never understand why I wasn't worthy of a kingdom.

A peasant who could not scrub of this misfortune of dark skin tone quick enough.

The media would define me as UGLY!

If not for my upbringing, I would not recover.

I learned to love myself.

 I learned to know that he made me in his image.

So no matter how dark I might be I couldn't be

dark enough.

I wear this proudly now.

It is who I am.

It is who my children will be.

I am beautiful.

-Lawrence E. B. Nicol

End of a Beautiful Era

I have a problem a problem.

Seems no one can help me with.

Every solution leads to a thought where I'd have

to quit loving you, but loving you is all that I'd

want to do.

Never ever thought this day would come.

It seems my world has ended.

And my Lord hasn't returned to take me home.

So what do I look forward to?

Every direction leads to you.

But I see nothing but dead ends.

I've lost my sense of smell.

Yet I smell that beautiful vanilla fragrance on your

heavenly skin.

I couldn't want to right a wrong more than this.

You are the reflection of my inner soul.

I look to better myself through you.

And without you my downward spiral is inevitable.

The words "I love you" don't do me justice.

I can't but help to want to reverse the hands of time.

I honestly believe my sole existence is to make sure you feel not one ounce of pain.

And to know the pain you felt was caused by me?

Truly is the most painful feeling in the world.

They say you never know what you have 'till it's gone.

But I've known for quite some time how much of a priceless woman you are.

Yet I've still managed to lose you.

Gambling with your heart will go down as my biggest regret.

I can only pray the next man will do right by you.

And no matter what I'll always be there to pick up the pieces.

If you need me to, until then I bid you adieu.

-Lawrence E. B. Nicol

Carved In Stone

I didn't really want to be this man.

My plan, it wasn't set in stone.

I loved her. I lost. I moved on.

Now when I hear our song

Memories leave me filled with despair.

Just a minute of her time

Brings an eternity of happiness.

Life stands still for no one.

Hating the ones you love is a painful feeling.

So I rejoice knowing I love the ones I hate.

There is no greater feeling than love.

So as I stare at the sky above,

I wish upon a star

That I never feel this feeling again.

Cause nothing hurts more than the betrayal of a
friend!

A friend that you once called lover.

-Lawrence E. B. Nicol

Gentlenigga

I guess I have to be a Gentlenigga.

Cause being a gentleman isn't good enough.

Since I treated you with respect,

You decided I wasn't hood enough.

Mistaking my kindness for weakness.

You bring the gentlenigga out of me.

Cause when I fuck you like I love you,

I'm the king of your world.

But if I love you like I fuck you,

It's just some bullshit ass words.

I don't claim to be perfect, but a gentleman I was.

Now I've transformed into this gentlenigga who

can't seem to give a fuck.

Cause being the nice guy no longer means the

right guy.

So I just gotta be the nigga.

So maybe if I punch you in the face you'll say you can't get enough of my nigga lovin'.

Baby I'll be gentle and console you, after I beat that ass!

I'll tell you no nigga could love you like I love you. This is true romance.

I will call you by the worst names... bitch and hoe, and only then will you understand how truly I go.

You can't leave me and you don't want to so I continue to smash.

You won't understand what it's like to be loved with this man.

Cause I'm a gentlenigga only concerned with getting mine and proving my manliness.

You weren't women enough for me to be a gentleman so I continue to dig your insides While you're wishing I knew the inner side of you instead of just getting inside you.

But a gentlenigga can't care for your feelings.

So as I'm breaking you off I just stare at the ceiling

Only a gentleman would stare you in your eyes as

if he loved you.

I'm a gentlenigga...you know I think I'm above you.

Just a sexual peasant, a human play toy.

I'll have you on some "back in the day when I was

young I'm not a kid anymore but some days I'll

make you wish you were a kid again" cause that'll

be the last time you remember being whole.

Being this gentlenigga, I've stripped you whole.

Mind, body, and soul.

No room to point fingers for my niggerish ways.

If you would have been a woman instead of a

bitch, it wouldn't happen this way.

I'll just be your gentlenigga until a better

gentlenigga comes your way.

-Lawrence E. B. Nicol

Lover's Slavery

Pride for shackles?

I can't seem to fathom

A world where you couldn't be mine.

It seems time's my only competition and it's the

one thing I'm running out of.

So patience is a thing of the past.

Anticipating a reunion is like waiting for the

second coming of Christ.

And you don't believe in God.

So where does that leave us?

With many miles between us?

It's becoming harder for you to remember me.

Harder for you to envision a world where we'd

Lay adjacent on pillow cases conversing the ills of

our day.

For now we're stuck with multimedia messages

that don't truly express our feelings.

Every day one click away to secure flights that
would solidify what once was.
But knowing that what once was is no longer
worthy of such an effort.
So I'll just wear my pride for shackles.

-Lawrence E. B. Nicol

My Nina Mosely

Doors open and legs spread.

Heaven and your skin synonymous.

You leave memories spread across pages.

Reciting words that left you numb for my touch.

Shouts and screams fill the room.

But all we hear is dead silence.

I'll pay attention to detail

So let me caress the parts of you most leave

undiscovered.

I could imagine you'd imagine this happening no

other way.

Open your eyes as I travel through you.

No passport needed to reach this destination.

Even though I'll fly through continents to reach

you.

Embrace this as if tomorrow wouldn't come.

As if this would be the last time I dine on your

sweetest treat.

Each kiss planted firmly.

Each kiss being better than the next.

All leading to the moment where we reach the tip

of Everest.

 And by all means please feel free to take this

journey again.

Cause I live for moments like this.

Seeking the thrill of the chase not knowing if I'll

ever catch you... Again.

-Lawrence E. B. Nicol

Who Will Intervene

I look at you and think I don't know what love is.

I don't know how I got here.

Wishing and hoping, not really praying, cause

I don't want God to intervene.

I want to see if you'll love me for me.

If you'll love me on your own.

Lost in what seems to be issues relating to trust.

Time flies but nothing really ever changes.

We've already gone through the motions and now

lovers became strangers.

We sit here confiding our inner most secrets to

some strangers.

I'm talking the facebooks and twitters of the

world.

Hoping they could bring some closure to these

open wounds.

Not knowing with each piece of misguided advice,

the cut just grows deeper.

And now we're drowning in a pool of blood.

Maybe now I'll ask God to intervene.

Cause I don't want to lose you.

But my grip on reality is running thin like the

blood through my veins.

I'm giving in to defeat only hoping you'll grab me

from my demise.

But you're stuck in the same position as me.

Cause you don't know what love is....

-Lawrence E. B. Nicol

Would You Believe

Would you believe that I still love you?

Yeah I wouldn't believe it either but I do.

Perfect pictures on broken canvases.

Is what our life's like... we couldn't separate the

good from the bad.

So we just basked in its misery.

Hoping tomorrow brings better days to come.

And though we may never meet at sunset,

We pray for the same direction but for different

things.

Realizing life's dreams aren't usually what they

seem.

I know you and I know you know me but still we

manage to never see

Eye to eye when face to face.

I can't help but wonder why but there's no

substance in the unexplained.

And I can't explain why you just don't love me the same.

I figured this would just be a temporary phase and we'd grow in days to come.

Not realizing we'd grow, but only further apart.

If only I could mirror your imperfections and make them my own.

If that would take less of a toll on you.

They say if you love something let it go.

If it comes back to you it was meant to be.

But who ever wonders what if you get lost on your journey?

The mind is a fickle being, and with so much to remember who's to say my love will take precedence.

In present tense... I can't make you love me that's evident.

But know my heart will never belong to another like it has to you.

Even though I'll never get it back the same.

I forgive you.

-Lawrence E. B. Nicol

Post 365

Almost a year later and your relevance lingers as if
our first kiss was 30 seconds prior.

I've removed you from my mind.

The struggles of letting go we know them so well.

Yet from time to time you pay me a visit.

And I welcome you with open arms.

As if all that has happened hadn't.

And we still revel in the idea of loving one
another.

But wise enough to know together is not where
we should be.

Though it'd be easy to point fingers and lay blame
upon ones doorstep.

What a disservice to the creator that would be.

He makes no mistakes.

So our time, if even short, played a purpose
beyond our control.

Who are we truly to sully a love whether it

be 3 months or 10 years?

Whatever he has given us we shall cherish it.

So know I no longer weep for you not being by my

side.

I hold my head high and beat my chest with pride.

I loved you whether the true casualty is that I use

that in past tense.

Or that I question daily if it should be present.

We'll never know....

-Lawrence E. B. Nicol

Love Bomaye (Kill Him)

You made a mockery of this love.

Dried tear ducts in the bosom of Manila.

Yet the smell of your flesh still haunts my nostrils.

How could I compete with a woman so godly.

I'd paid tithes to the devil for a fighting chance .

Yet you still tip toed around the ring like God was

your cut man.

The odds were forever in your favor.

Though we'd go blow for blow,

It's evident you got me.

I could work the ropes in hopes that

I'd muster up some strength to defeat you.

But I already let my guard down

PROTECT YOURSELF AT ALL TIMES!

The lesson learned after the lesson taught.

Now I face a ten count to the end of it all.

You WIN love, you beat me.

-Lawrence E. B. Nicol

The End

23775026R00062

Made in the USA
Middletown, DE
02 September 2015